Limitless Humanity

Anna Bond

BookLeaf
Publishing

Presentation by *BookLeaf Publishing*

Web: www.bookleafpub.com

E-mail: info@bookleafpub.com

ISBN: 9789357213479

First edition 2023

feat of origin

rippling of tide, a trickle in orbit
rough rigidity stilling all might
loop into the self, consume respiration
sink down the spine - origin

visible, disintegrated, i know not
pleasure, pain, symptoms of thought
spirals extend divinity endlessly on
shockingly exposing all burials to dawn

refusal runs short, surrender to feat
grasp nothing but loosely, refract
rising and falling, water moves forward
for streams are channeling bodies - mundane

you are limitless

i feel on the verge.
as if i am always
a breath away
from being pushed

over the edge-
except the edge never comes closer
it remains barely out of sight-
never emerging

perhaps that is what growth is.
constantly being pushed to your limit
just to learn
that you are limitless

never the same again

down into the river i row
moving deeper into the flow
forward nor backward find me here
deeper i hide from my fear

my fear of finding what i left,
left and shut behind with a slam
or rowing wayward-
too wayward for return

returns happen never
for myself whom was yesterday
is gone forever
rowing they died and re-birthed

now their name represents more
but also less
something new and altogether
never the same again

returning, have i

have i climbed from a grave
i packed densely above
among flowers having nothing
but the cold to chill them

wilting and drying they
crumbled and thinned to be
as fair as a last breath
possessed only by stillness

words mean so much and
so little. the sobs never cried
only now brake the surface
for the fight to life meant most

returning, am i to the stillness
only found in the passionate
purity of a soul shouting out
returning, am i?

thankful, i am

clarity, i find in the sobs
the ones that create themselves
those are true and unquestionably
affirming of my soul direction

for what i long for most
my chest heaves unbarably towards
as if it recognizes no authority
of my mind that restricts it

restricted my sobs know not
but pushing stronger to the surface
their fight is all they have
to live and leave unrest

thankful i am.
my mind deceives me, the truth
it tells has the weight of the air
i often grasp and fall empty

self is slain

living, i see now
is what i have wanted
reviving, i have been trying
for too long, but no more

my life i begin
with the ease of my sins
as they teach me and
leave me human

i see now i died
many times inside for
the people i cared and
could not live without

living i must for dead
they surely won't stay
it matters never if my
love for self is slain

union in pressing

slowly, measurably i placed
each step. my heel pressed,
my arch stretched, and
my toes tensed into edges.

edges of gravel that fit
into the next like friends
they had unity and moved
still as flesh weighed down

slowly a pattern emerged
into spirals in and around
the surface packed down, far
embedded spirals in gravel.

i wonder how deeply the
ground feels these wounds
is the union in pressing seen
as art or pain-filled wounds?

i am walking

backwards i am walking
to what i hated most
shutting out what hurt me,
i hurt me the most

backwards i am walking
into the shadows i created
of pockets like wounds
gaping and gasping for care

backwards i am walking
to meet again those pieces
of myself i could not see
which needed love most

forward i walk with my
shadows rowed into a line
side by side we embrace
knowing only love and light

goodbye terrifies

love and heal, these words
i dream into the cords
i cut lose in a rage of
fear and desperation born.

many i have left behind
funny saying goodbye terrifies
most myself to ice while
i leave the most damage behind

fear, i should say goodbye
then hello again to mend
i seek only to recognize and
own the tares i wish see thin.

back again we are to see

back again we are to see
each other's lives unfold
speak to me your finest dreams
heart racing, embody to thrive

shocked, charged, electrified
these visions do call your soul
affirm and become, you will,
for not, both night and day haunt

become you, already planted
warm love, water with a knowing
sprout the leaves, find expression
give energy, time, life

back again, we are to see
each other's lives unfold
across the sea, our past lives beam
lessons across time align, bloom.

bloomed, have i, without realizing

bloomed, have i, without realizing
the truth i hold full, tall and wide
the space my edges hold inside
and expand past all binding

heavy no more, i am finding
lightness; no idea, had i
how heavy i was, for this sight
lays dormant for past reflections

past weights have dissolved
with love i find release and
with contrast i know of ease
allowing fluidity of gold within

bloomed, have i, without realizing,
or have i always reached so fully
conversing with the sun goddess above
and only now recollect, aware

disorientation within the cycles

changing things are, shifting always
you can hear it, like sand funneling
it stirs and blends, but what
is one single grain alone?

a beach lays inside my ribs
the ocean pumps away and returns
my life i have spent wishing to
identify each grain i am made from

the grains move and become lost,
covered and swept away.
my dreams, desires, labels, obessions,
if i lose one, do i lose them all?

disorientation within the cycles
identifying one, remaining forever
this does not exist. they all move
with universal law holding center.

you saw my lie

at the end, a hug was given
strangers we were, but perhaps not
a supportive embrace i knew not
i needed as a heart's scream ended

nothing in return was given, for
i did not grasp too tightly to this
person i knew not with my acts of
service: a disguised codependency

hunted and haunted, you showed again
you saw my truth, my cry for help
calm and collected, i hide in this.
i never need, but you saw my lie

again i see and search for you in my
dreams where i first met you.
black hair i see as you shift, touching
a glowing berry grown from tree, magic

breathe sacred

classifications and analyzations
why is it i feel that others possess the
need to give diagnoses of ailments
they see in me like i know nothing

is this a way humans have grown
addicted to the shoveling away of self
improvement under layers of societal
guilt and strife for synthetic perfection

let us have a conversation and
recognize my self contentment
not as ignorance and blinders, but
with love and ease i breathe sacred.

digging into thyself is to perpetuate.
mangling the perfect imperfections i find
only cuts and scrapes pieces of my soul
that could instead be shifting into light

detached.

detached and falling, feeling nothing
but the depth of emptiness inside.
body supported by earth but skin is
slack, unhinged are the heart and mind.

familiar i am of this process of holding
emptiness as i drop any emotion or
thought or blindingly painful cry for
love to the wind for the sake of peace.

if i embraced myself, i fear i would ruin
us in a blaze; pop and thwack against
all loved dear in the efforts to tell how
much i care as you run away and hide.

to you anew

a break, that is what this feels of.
separation, independence, as if we
are drifting on diverging paths and
calling long distance in the same bed

a lot has happened in the eleven days
since you spoke of focusing on yourself
a time of ending my sharing of wounds,
of thoughts, of time, of intimate hearts

a loft the idea was to me, that my
sculpture of raw connection created the
bars that made prisoner and rusting-
an internal itch held unseen for too long.

free now we lay lost to both the self and other
hand in hand with nothing to hold.
I dream to become my higher self, the one
who has been introduced to you anew.

i will wait for you

i hold to silence though against
my nature: fire so warm, nurturing,
fluidly creating all that is bright, and,
for us, our babies a loyal, secure home.

for you i will hold my voice within while it
grows and shines for my own sake and others.
mistake as goodbye, you should not.
i will wait for you to speak aloud:

i love you, bare to me your soul.

the same

sit in intuition. reflect the waters
made vulnerably visible, for we
are all a piece of the same oneness.
different perspectives of source
within and entangled of universe.

eased i am

clammy palms, erratic beating
my heart strings are pulled.
options, time, location, connections
never knowing how the future unfolds.

dare i say to follow my wishes
anxiety crawls, the vocals escape yes.
crazy, lost, impulsive others will say
as i clear the path never walked

dream, believe, all will unfold
i take the leap and eased i am
finally i choose to believe not them
but say yes to who i have always been

beyond societal validations, i seek
endless exploration of cultures,
worlds, and the ancient mysteries-
endless and dependably constant.

the healthiest i have felt in years
i breathe comforting air as tension
of squeezing into molds release
divinely guided, no longer just surviving.

ellis

ellis,
we walked
side by side
carrying
two angels.
in harmony
with mother
earth, all
was love
and unity.
remember
to nurture
divinity
and truly,
simply
just be.

wholesome intensity

wholesome intensity- it is a different sort
the sort that flares in an instant
its an exchange within a gaping, raw innocence
the flutter of a silhouette, a voice
a longing to be present together
it's of a quickening flux
energy increases to a forever state
the physical panics
a good sort of quake
the kind that rejects reality
engulfed
in the remembrance
of what it feels
to be home

www.ingramcontent.com/pod-product-compliance
Lightning Source LLC
Chambersburg PA
CBHW062112140826
49812CB00058B/1310
9789357213479